Only the Brave

Uttara Desai

BookLeaf Publishing

India | USA | UK

Presentation by *BookLeaf Publishing*

Web: www.bookleafpub.com

E-mail: info@bookleafpub.com

ISBN: 9789363311190

First edition 2024

Heart Tantrums

In subdued submission,
among tamed revision,
between hell and earth,
I suffered.

With man surrounded by dreams,
through illuminating beams.
To emblematise answered prayers,
to comprehend repairs,
with clouds unstained,
I sustained.

In pragmatic sustenance,
among echoed dissonance,
between earth and heaven,
I survived.

Unuttered Faith

Moment after moment, hour after hour,
day after day, year after year.
I waited all along,
just to see Him.

I held myself close to time,
just to surrender all of mine,
little did I know I was where,
He had made a heaven there.

Step after step, door after door,
breath after breath, beat after beat.
My heart knew, I was where,
My soul was there.

Unpronounced Miracle

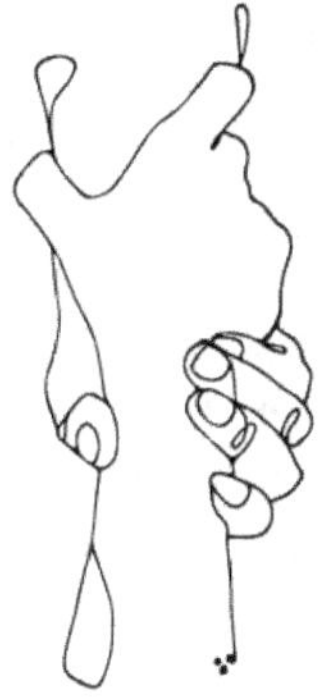

Stepped into His abode, only to realise,
it was not me, but always Thine.
It was always Thine,
that which I was tricked to be mine.

I shivered, I trembled,
I struggled to breathe.
My heart gasped at every beat.
Oh, what a miracle to see,
all fearsome elements free.

Tears rolled down my cheeks,
I knew no time, nor me.
I knew but Him, he was there,
to hold my hand, I need him there.

To me He is Faith,
to me He is God,
to me He is everything,
without Him I am lost.

I believed Him, I always will.
I trusted Him, I always will.
He held my hand when I was weak,
He holds my hand when I seek.

Pleasant Notice

To what do I owe this blessing,
To the Universe or to Him.
For he came and stood right before me,
and I knew not myself nor me.

His grace, my only solace,
His hands mean so much to this novice.
He knows life to amalgamate all elements,
He knew me to care for my sentiments.

I trust Him more,
more than anything.
To find Him at my worst,
blessed I am with many things.

Oh, sweet nature! Oh, his sweet nurture!
Resting in delight brushing my worries,
He caresses my life while he spells sureties.

Untamed Hope

Banishing morning sunshine,
there was no rest in moonshine,
the body trembled, it curled in fear,
the face revealed darkness was near.

I shook, I pushed,
I shunned, I looked.
At the unfortunate fine,
it was there to take all of mine.

Resisting the thunder,
there she was, another wonder.
She rose above me,
to all my pain, my only key.

I thought, I pondered,
I felt, I wandered.
At the edge of hope,
it stood there to help me cope.

Unforgotten Courage

Nurturing the inner peace,
mending the broken piece.
To look up at the sky,
awaiting a reply.

It took courage to get help,
it took love to shun the yelp.
Lying over still water of fire,
life demanded to rise higher.

Spelling the inner silence,
carrying a demilance.
To climb the steep slope,
grabbing the rope.

It took courage to spell hope,
it took care to pronounce cope.
Running over beads on soft grass,
faith instructed for the pain to surpass.

Rooted Assertion

I know, you will be well.

I know you will smile,
I know you will share.
I know, you care.

Were my fear as small,
you held when I called.
You were the strength and so you are,
you are as then, never so far.

The wind knows you are strong, you heal.
The universe knows you fight bold, it pleads.

Eyes wandered just to find you,
morning, noon, evening, night.
Heart called, just to see you,
your voice gave me the love I sight.

I know, I know, you be well.
I know, I know, hear me well.

Unclouded Dreams

Cape of victory, golden shawl too,
I see it, I have to.
Cape of glory, the book of fineness,
to none but me, embracing primness.

Apt in red, glitters of golden, walk to and sit to
pray.
Braids and flowers, scents of sandal.
He blesses me, you be there.
I know, I know, you, love, will be there.

Fight strong, fear not.
I once fought, you saw me,
you now fight, demands He.
You stand with courage,
tall and strong as ever.
You encourage,
let the world know this is forever.

Believe in the universe, it knows the best.
It understands you, your powers in it rest.

12

Expressed Union

What do I owe to the universe?

Showcasing the colour of sunbeams,
sensing the glory that one seems.
Smelling the haze in nature's air,
showing the courage to share.

Walking over uncoiled roots,
kissing the imperfect disputes.
Inhaling the morning's dew,
bowing to the magical muse.

To embrace reality, or to create eternity?
to shun the noise, or to hear the joys?

What do I owe to the universe?
In its deep, calm, warm waters, to forever
immerse.

Nature's Hymn

Expressing emotions, chirping of the birds,
nurturing priced relations, a flower's first words.
Laying over wet grass, under the sky as glass,
say yes to connection, utter the sense of
protection.

Knowing the universe has your back,
nature in it heals the messy cracks.
Noticing the trees get ready for the spring,
life in it cuts the uncherished strings.

Dream big, said the mountains,
be ecstatic, like the fountains.
Flow smooth, whispered the streams,
stay alive, witnessed the regimes.

Nurturing nature's finest gems,
treasuring them in newly born stems.
Uttering union, such with the divine,
resting in profound pain, ageing as the wine.

Water and Earth

Dwelling in steady rush, making nature blush,
water narrated its story, showcasing the earth's
glory.
He heard with careful ears, stories from years,
that stillness taught him, that earth knew to
swim.

Pronouncing the rare elements,
they nurtured nature's sentiments.
To flow or to stay, they knew their way.
To dance or to meditate, they never hesitate.

Laying on a delicate cloud, avoiding the crowd,
Earth spoke in praise, water his only gaze.
He whispered to her peace,
she found her awaited release.

Oh, a bond so pure!
Like the night sky's urge to converge with
morning's light,
like water's urge to spell earth in quiet.
Innate to nature's embrace, a profound trace.
Fragrance bought by water's grace, earth's only
safe place.

Escape, not escape

Surfing through high tides,
rushing through barren paradise.
Shadowed silence of the moon,
made the gem look gloom.

Resting at an innocent shore,
I heard his footsteps soar,
to grab my fragile arm,
to save me from unsettling harm.

His voice, his words, his skies, and my cries.
Oh, so fine, to heal all of mine.

Whilst we cherished the unknown,
and sky knew not the lone.
For blossoms that which last forever,
seldom bow to time, said the narrator.

Boundless Ocean

Growing with timeless ecstasy,
moving past unplanned fantasy,
near the shore of uncertainty,
he gave me the promise of eternity.

Laughters that pronounce future,
warmth such like to nurture,
near the shore of hope,
he gave me a reason to cope.

Through the window to the soul,
it seemed to me a magical stroll.
Whilst I believe in hope,
life seems to me now, a blessed note.

Subtle Heaven

It was dark, it was bright,
mesmerizing in awe to write.
Entering with a glimpse of elegance,
departing with a source of vibrance.

Colours, here and there,
Marbles, a sheath of history.
Antiques, here and there,
past, a prayer to mystery.

Quite, silent, and calm,
fireflies of peace hold my arm.
Dark, clear, and patterned,
skies gather the scattered.

Treasures of majestic breath, surpassing death.
Why a story and not a glory?
Why so subtle and a puzzle?

Spelt Realities

I knew, I existed in those walls.
I knew I had touched, the history calls.

To what do I owe my love?
To now can I live my love?
To the next time.
The next time.

Entering a realm of connection,
breathing the air of affection.
Accepting the beauty of dignity,
gracing the elegance in eternity.

History, an unaccounted myth, they say.
Story, a spelt reality, I say.

Unheard Roar

Identity is in us all along,
like a moon treasuring its lone song.
Imagining the rustic wind recollect,
the sea guides our intellect.

Identity is such a maze,
mind's control is just a haze.
Untamed spirit in it resides,
liberate it and it subsides.

The sun shone and the waves roared,
like holy water, they poured.
The birds sang and the wind blew,
like identity, they all drew.

Yet, it must be dissolved,
for us to be involved.

Untold Silence

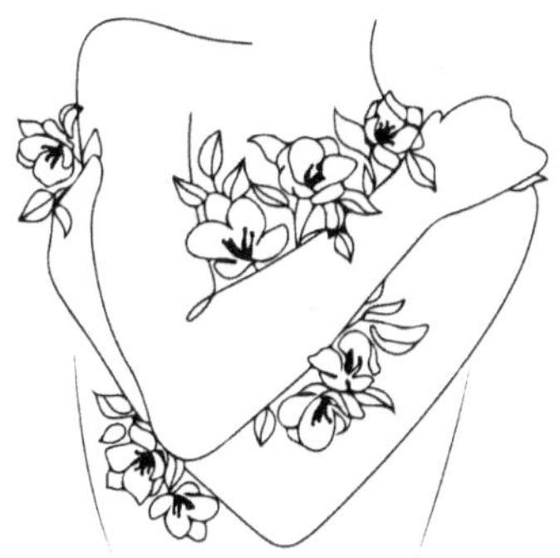

Drop by drop, flower by flower,
they all came to exist as if in an hour.
Took a leap wondering what it stored,
the heart of nature or its roar.

Little by little, step by step,
he saw them as if kept.
The chaos, the silence,
there was so much at each step.

The pleasant sky, embracing the earth.
The raindrops, reciting melody.
To what do we owe this remedy,
To them or the Mirth.

Tender was nature to sense her inclusion,
One by one, she spoke liberation.

Treasured Sea

They were pearls,
they knew why waves curl.
As white as a dove,
they knew love.

Pearls they were,
keeping silence here for.
To treasure the echo of the sea,
holding nature's intimate key.

They were precious,
not among the semi-precious.
The girl who nurtured, saw them not cultured.
It was wondrous, calming the world so
thunderous.

Untangling them for liberation,
braiding them for creation.

Free Horizons

Gazing at timeless travels,
exploring the magic life unravels,
I stood before time asking why,
why does it not plead the sky?

To map the horizons,
to cure the wizened.
To ask nature,
to plead for its nurture.

Time heals, they say.
Ask the sky to open its arms,
it would take you in, to cure every harm.

Unhinged Faith

She would whisper words of love;
like a flight slides through the curve,
she would ensure you pronounce love.

Still as the clouds, navigating the sky.
Bold as an eagle, scaling the horrendous why.

Surrender to her grandeur, she knows what you
need,
you will nudge stillness, to your soul you'll feed.

Aware is the Universe

Walking past unsettling times,
recognizing the subtle signs.
He knocks the door when you ask,
when you wish, let's surrender the mask.

He who knows you can,
He who makes the plan.
Oh, so not bothered if you know,
to take life just so slow.

Oh, a life so slow!
You rest in its very flow.
Oh, a life you explore!
You rest at the shore.

Ancient Wisdom

Resting your breath in nature's name,
oblivious to all the fame.
You breathe, like the morning dew,
You live, like the mountain in your view.

A mountain so majestic and bold,
a forest so vast and old.
In it you will find your truest self,
you will discover yourself.

Love that person for life is too short,
learn to embrace the rusty distort.
It is in them that life spells,
Ancient wisdom, oh, the world dispels.
You welcome the world's ignored chase,
for nature to provide its warm embrace.

Constant Need

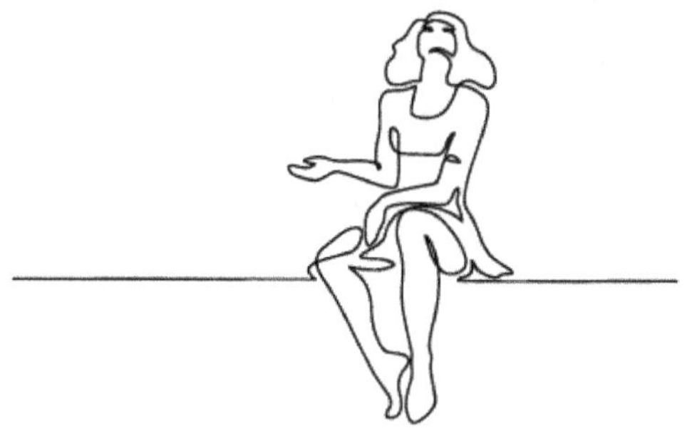

In life's rugged sustenance,
in combating dominance,
we often fail to realise,
our life, we trivialize.

Our strength to fight,
our zeal to hold on tight,
our dream to breathe free,
our constant urge to rest under a tree.

The chaotic chatter,
the endless pitter-patter,
the soar heart,
the unhealed art.

It shuns the bloom, only to make everything so
gloom.
To that soul we plead,
understand that Peace is our breath's constant
need.

Mirth

In a world of suppressed silence, can I breathe?

Can I breathe on a dusty summer afternoon?
Can I kiss the full moon?
Can I take the troubled mind of mine to meet my
pleasant soul?
Can I ever feel enough and whole?

I pondered and met the stars,only to ask them,
Where's the gem?
A gem that shines bright,
a gem never scared to fight.

Oh, in their glorious sparkles they met my eye,
I saw in them the sky.
I saw the world, fondly called Earth,
I saw love take birth.

Love is the true gem, the only gem.
for love gives birth to Mirth,
for love rests in the lap of Earth.
She takes care of us all,
She understands what it is to fall,
by the hands of those who showcase their care,
only in the disguise of repair.

Pleasant Error

For when life frowns,
our hope in it drowns.
To forgo the past,
know the shadows it cast.

To know that our dreams are shattered,
you see pieces of your heart scattered.
You hurt yourself gathering what's broken,
when your hands are cold, why fear the frozen?

Look up, smile bright.
Look down, your feet are ready to fight.
If only there was an option,
to read and narrate the signs of caution.

Unheard dreams voice the error,
that life made, oh, Sweet Heaven! It was just
being clever.

Journey through

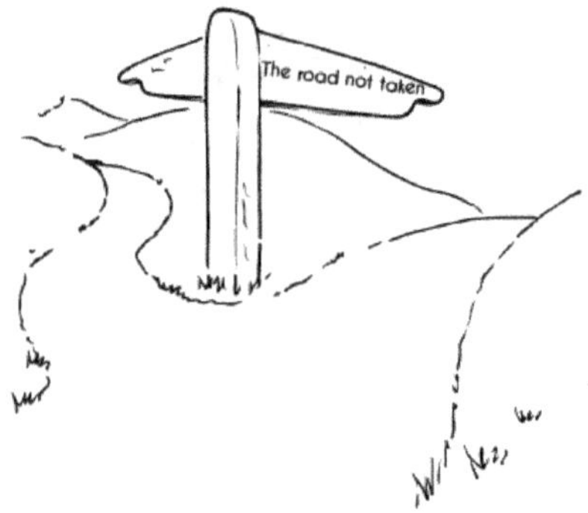

Gathering profound courage,
take life to encourage.
To collect what's true to your nature,
to put down that which whispers denature.

Showcasing patience to comprehend,
ponder on thoughts that blend.
With your raw self; when you dissolve yourself.
In sights that respond,
in sounds that whisper, go beyond.
In touch; oh, as if you are the most precious
pearl,
in fragrance, in its embrace you curl.

Embracing your innermost fears,
caressing your every tear,
in it lies the strength to discover,
our lost hopes in it we recover.

Fruitful Disguise

Oh, the morning dew,
the moments you find few.
In life that tests you,
it lets you pursue.

Oh, the things you love, like thyself,
Oh, the things that make your heart race, like
love itself.
Oh, the things you desire,
Oh, the things that inspire.

Know it all while you have it none,
know it like you know the setting sun.
Like it diffuses aware about its rise,
you take life, let sadness in disguise.
For when it reveals itself,
you assert your rise thyself.

Settling Rest

The settling calmness.
The unsettling rupture.
Let your heart not capture,
only that chapter.

Let it not shun your soul,
let it not only console.
Your grieving heart,
your incomplete art.

Let it revive your broken piece,
let it help you release.
That which is not true,
that which is not for you.

Know that heart knows the best,
it knows when to give thyself some rest.

www.ingramcontent.com/pod-product-compliance
Lightning Source LLC
La Vergne TN
LVHW010929200726
843509LV00013B/2144